Evoke

Yash Gaur

Made with ❤ on the BookLeaf Publishing Platform
www.bookleafpub.in
www.bookleafpub.com

Dedication

To my family, whose love and unwavering support have shaped the person I am today. To my teachers, who nurtured my curiosity and helped me find my voice through their wisdom and guidance. And lastly to my friends, who have shared with me the highs and lows of life, enriching my understanding of the world.

Preface

For some, this book has nothing and for others it has everything. It's your eye that'll decide it. You may find it to be a handbook to life, a lyric to the music that plays in your heart, or a mere collection of letters from a broken man. I hope when you pick this, you approach it with an open mind. Because if you do - you may experience madness, intoxication, highs, warmth and cold. At every turn of the page, you may find a reflection of your deepest, darkest thoughts or an expression of the joy and elation of life.

The objective of this book is not to impose my thoughts on the reader. Neither it is to seek their validation. The objective of this book is to be. And in doing so, maybe, to help someone find a feeling of belonging, to feel inspired and express, and seek comfort in being who they are.

In the remarkable words of the legendary Freddie Mercury:

"You can do what you want with my music but don't make me boring."

Acknowledgements

The contents of this book are a consequence of my experiences with life. And what is life made up of? People. People raise you and bring you down. They shape your perceptions and the foundation of who you are. This book wouldn't exist without certain names that made it possible.

I am extremely grateful to these people for contributing to my growth and making me who I am. My muse, my wife - Vinushka - who always admired my philosophical side and kept that flame from extinguishing. My friend, Bhupendra, who always encouraged me to write. My parents, Paresh and Shubha, who shaped me as an individual. My sibling, Yashvi, who was always there for me in her own subtle ways.

This acknowledgement would be incomplete without the many names that inspired the thoughts that are reflected in this book. I hope when they read it, they know that they made an equal contribution.

1. Camera Roll

Holding negatives against the light;
photographs in the wallet;
giggling at the paper plane's flight;
I want aliens from a different time.
Polaroids hanging down their walls;
waiting at the booth for a phone call.

Love letters between the books;
rose smudges on the pages;
holding memories in paper albums,
Movies on a disc, music in a cassette;
turn off the internet and find me a radio.
I'll kiss you as we back our car onto the patio.

Time is an ever-flowing river
and I hang by a hook.
Let's go fishing to the forgotten brook,
wearing our skin and taking a dive,
Drenching our hair in the juice of life.

Rolled down windows, sunset drives,
A cup of coffee when your <u>cottage</u> arrives.
No hook ups but a kiss of goodbye
Then making love for the rest of our lives.

Find me aliens from a different time,
a dusty old record of a morning chime,
to look back at a life of wild adventure
and laugh like kids at nursery rhymes.

2. Circles

Life rolls around.
Moments flash by
in seconds of time,
when the tide turns around
leaving behind the ringing sound.

The little fingers hold you tight;
you are a safe haven;
you are hope.
Don't you leave love behind.
It comes by once;
Life's little phase of fun.
She'll ask you how did I know,
Tell her for me that the wind told me so.

I'd love to stay,
but I have to go
The tide will take me away.
I want you to hold on
and let the <u>wind</u> know.

I was here, and
my life was an adventure
She'll ask you how did I know,
tell her for me that I told you so.

3. Paper Planes

Boeing and Air Bus rides are all fine
But if life allows,
I'd like to get back
that <u>ticklish</u> feeling
from witnessing that sight
of paper planes
made from notebook pages
make their first flight.

4. Treasure Island

They found a map to a treasure island
So they set sail on their mighty young wings.

They crossed the sea in an ancient boat
and built a camp on the island's shore.

In their hunt for gold, they looked around;
crossed the valley and dug the ground.
And till midnight they toiled together,
But the ancient treasure was never found.

Tired, they lay on the island's beach,
gazing at the stars they wanted to reach.
And in that moment of rare peace,
they heard the secret the island keeps.

"Oh! How us fools spent a lifetime,
chasing the glittering pleasure.
When our love is the gold
and this moment is the treasure."

5. Young Blood

Let me write our story in young blood.
I'll read it out to you one day
through spectacled eyes
in a cozy bed, on a wintery night.
While you'll peer out the foggy windows
and our love will glitter in its twilight.

6. Moments

Holding on to moments
is like holding on to sand.

One second you have them in your
grasp, the next you find them
slipping out of your hand.

7. More than Three Words

Love isn't
always found as
three magical
words.

Sometimes it's
in the form of
'text me when
you reach home'.

Sometimes in the
form of a long
wait while
staring at your
phone.

8. Winter Dew

You know
the feeling
that you get
when you walk
bare feet,
on the grass
covered in
winter morning dew?

When you'll look
into her eyes
she'll give
the same feeling to you.

9. Soulmates

Isn't it amazing?
The strange connection
that we find in a stranger's heart.
And though it's difficult
for the eyes to recognize the face,
the <u>souls</u> somehow know that
they've met before in a different age.

10. Sober and High

There was a moonlit road
that went through the woods.
We walked on it with tipsy steps,
holding hands under the starry sky.
And by the time we reached its end,
she was sober, I was high.

11. Lullaby

I don't wish for the fancy stuff
Just the basics will do
Rarely but certainly there'll be days
when I will call upon you

So when the radio won't play
The songs that ease my pain
Will your laughter be my lullaby?

When I'll be driving through the night
With no strength left inside
Will your voice be my respite?

One day when my GPS will fail
will you stay on the phone
Till I find out a way?

And when I won't be at my best
Will you allow me to rest

Listening to the music that comes
from the middle of your chest?

12. The One in Dreams

I wonder
where you'd been before,
the wonderland where
glimmering waves
kiss the shore.

Under the golden aubade
of the sun
or moonlight's silver gleam.
Oh! now I know you are the one
I had seen in dreams.

13. Ecstasy and Heartbreaks

I have lived a life
in ecstasy
and heartbreaks.

One took me
to a wonderland
and the other
shook me to reality.

14. Masks

When I gaze in the mirror
there's a figure that I see.
I ask the mirror if that is me.

"I do not know," the mirror says,
"I haven't seen your real face.
There are <u>masks</u> you wear throughout the day
for the different roles in life you play."

15. Canvas

Let me splash your soul
with my words,
let me help them see
what their eyes never found.

I'll paint your sketch
in a certain way;
It will be a mirror
but more profound.

The calm that you are
will be shown with blue;
Violet for the tempest
that lies within you.

The <u>fire</u> that you have
will be marked with red.
And black will show
you're as true as Death.

16. Queen

Have you ever met a queen?
She is not like the ones
that you find in fairy tales
or in Disney princess diaries.

She is the kind
that you will find
in a game of Chess.
Sweeping across the battlefield,
Causing dread in the enemy ranks.
And while you'll figure out your move,
Her moves will command your fate
In white she'll be there to save your ass
And in black she'll be your checkmate.

17. The Secret She Holds

She hides a thousand secrets
behind her smile;
that smile is the greatest
of all her lies.

There's a story untold
in her heart that she keeps;
the story you would read
when you'd dive into her eyes.

18. The Peace in Her Thoughts

She was the calmness
to my wild soul
after all the violent battles
with itself it has fought.

I knew it when
she induced in me
a certain madness
and I found peace
in her toxic thoughts.

19. The Poet Came from the Pain

There's a part of my soul,
engraved with words
that were forged in passion's flame.
The ink was drawn from my blood;
the poet came from the pain.

20. Inferno and Grace

Such passion did her eyes ignite,
The Devil fell for the Angel that night,
His love was pure, his reality was grim,
The Devil knew she'll never be with him,
For she was the solace that mortals desire,
And he was the fury of Inferno's fire,
Why you may ask does it put me to peril,
'Cause you're that Angel and I am the Devil.

21. Judgement Day

Carved by the Devil, the darkness of world,
I was made of poison and blood,
I once was lost but never was found,
In the echoes of war, its deafening sound.

My name is no one, the long lost sun
Raised with the stories of heroes and Gods,
That left me for dead and went for a run.

The scars on my hands, the slash on my back,
Is all that I now have to show.
I gathered my pride and I choked on my faith,
But I gave her my heart and my soul.

I challenged the Death, I made a bouquet
Out of flowers left over my grave,
While I sit in the waiting room writing this song,
Preparing for another battle, preparing
for Judgement Day.

22. Call from the Coffin

I am tired of sleeping in my grave;
the darkness is suffocating.
I am waiting for someone
to move my tombstone.
To let me crawl out from my dungeon.
I want to see the broad daylight,
the morning dawn,
the wintery sunset vibe.

Let the sunlight burn my flesh
I want to feel the dew
when the night lays it on the grass afresh.

Let me live this one more time.
I will be more wise;
I'll waste no time;
I'll make love to life
wildly and for long.
I'll hike to that mountaintop
singing this song.

There's no life after life;
all that remains is foul and decay.
Of the dried roses the beloved leave
and the dead ones they lay.

Breathe, breathe one more time;
look more often to the bright blue sky.
I'll be a bird, I don't need any wings,
My heart was mortal but my soul will fly.

I wanna love love, one more time,
redo it all that's left behind.
I wanna leave my footprints
on the sands of time,
for the dead to follow back
and find the divine.

It took me death to figure it out -
It seems life runs from forward to rewind.
There's an empty space
between the pyre and paradise
only the pyre lies ahead and
the paradise is left behind.
That's what life has become to be,
I want to run backwards one more time.

23. Changes

I dread closed envelopes,
unseen messages, unheard knocks
moving cities; finding new docks.
I dread the letter that's still unread,
the paths untread; the worn out thread;
new beginnings and old endings;
new places, new faces, old traces
I dread changes.

An old library,
turning its yellow tinted pages;
living life in stages;
burning cages,
in hope of turning back to old ages.
I dread turning pages
to a broken chapter.
I dread changes.

Stay here, stay the same.
It's strange.

I can't change.
I can't quench this burning rage.
It's said I hold on to you so tight.
I dread winter nights;
the sound of the silence
with no moonlight.

The changing faces of the moon;
waiting for the impeding doom;
echoes in the vacant room;
walking past my dusty tomb
in the afterlife.
with no stories to tell;
no places to dwell;
no one to call home;
no pending texts on the phone.

I dread changing seasons;
unreasonable reasons;
promises and treasons.

So, when the morning comes,
I must grab the reigns
and ride away into the rain.
It's inevitable, unstoppable, unquenchable.
It's time, I rewrite this fable:
It's time to break away our dance;

It's time I shake myself from your trance;
It feels strange though: to free the chains
It feels strange though: it'll be a change.

24. Rapunzel

She won't ask you
to find her missing shoe,
or be someone
who wishes for flowers.

For she's Rapunzel;
she'll be the queen
to her own castle,
and when you'll call upon
she'll fetch you up to its tower.

25. Dear Deer

Dear deer don't you run away
I have left behind the bow and arrow;
I am just a wanderer in this forest
Sniffing the roots of life's marrow.

Dear deer don't you weep;
We'll rub it off on the pillow
After a good night's sleep.

Although the nights are scary,
we'll persist in the hope
of watching a sunny day.
We'll light a fire under the tree
to keep the tiger away.

I will watch out for you
when the forest puts us to test.
I hope you won't hesitate
With your antlers when I stop to rest.

Dear dear, let's keep them sharp,
Your antlers and my broken harp;
We have to reach before its dark
To be in time for the waiting ark.

We'll make it through in hasty leaps
As Frost echoes in the forest deep -
'We have got promises to keep
and miles to go before we sleep.'

26. The World of Imagination

We must be grateful for
the power of imagination
that we possess.
There's a world where
we can be what we are
and where life can be
how we want it to be.

27. A Heart of Gold

How erroneously to us
have they told,
a story and proverb
of times old,
a heart that loves
is not that of gold,
'cause gold can't love,
it's dead and cold.